A CODER LIKE me

WRITTEN BY

Dr Shini Somara
WITH *Catherine Coe*

ILLUSTRATED BY

Nadja Sarell

wren
&rook

"I think we're going to have fun today, Sam!" says Auntie Jo.

Sam is staying at Auntie Jo's house for the day.

Sam's eyes boggle at all the gadgets and computers in her office.

"What's your job, Auntie Jo?" Sam asks.

"I'm a coder! That means I tell computers what to do."

"Computers need instructions?" Sam didn't know that!

"Yes – they won't work without them. Computers need ALGORITHMS, which are a list of steps to follow in order to solve a problem. Just like real life, really!"

"Huh?"

"Take getting ready for school in the morning..."

Your alarm goes off to wake you up.

You turn off the alarm, get up and have a wash.

Then you get dressed,

have breakfast

and clean your teeth.

You have to do all of these things to be ready for school — and in the right order!

Jo grins. "Talking of breakfast, would you like some porridge?"

"We are surrounded by computers of all shapes and sizes, even in the kitchen," Jo explains. "Like this microwave! Can you spot any others?"

Microwave

Radio and speakers

Fridge

Freezer

Smartwatch

"These objects are called 'hardware'. What I do is code the 'software', which tells the hardware what to do."

After breakfast, Jo takes Sam into the garage.

"Look at this circuit board. The switches turn on and off, using a basic code that's called binary, which uses just 0s and 1s. If a switch is 1, it is on. If a switch is 0, it is off."

At first, computer codes used only numbers and symbols, but Grace Hopper created the first code that used words.

In the 1960s, she decided that people shouldn't need to know a complicated set of symbols to program computers. She created the computer language COBOL, which allows people to write programs in English and computers to then translate the English into code.

Sam peers over the circuit board.
"What are those black things?"

"Electronic chips!" says Jo.

"Chips have millions of gates in order to do complex work. There are chips that create the graphics on a computer screen, chips that have lots of memory for saving data, and chips that run the computer's programs."

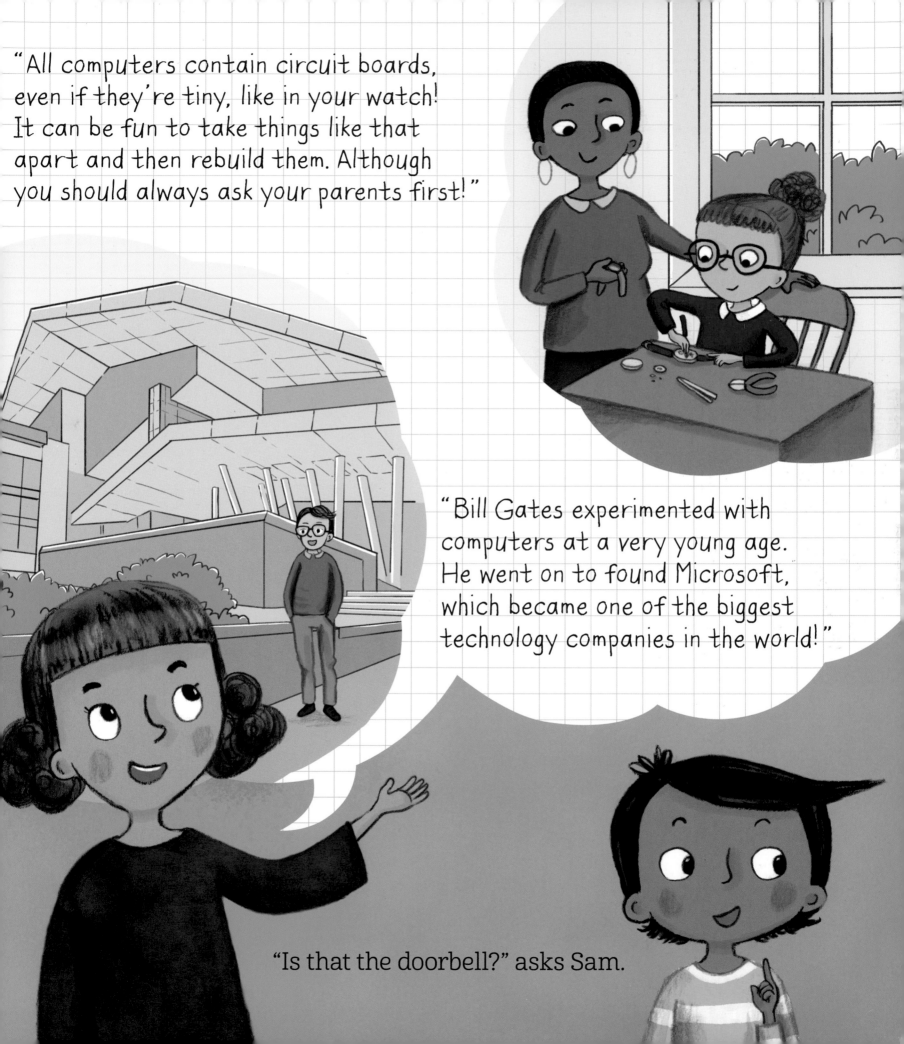

"All computers contain circuit boards, even if they're tiny, like in your watch! It can be fun to take things like that apart and then rebuild them. Although you should always ask your parents first!"

"Bill Gates experimented with computers at a very young age. He went on to found Microsoft, which became one of the biggest technology companies in the world!"

"Is that the doorbell?" asks Sam.

They rush back into the house, but there's no one at the door. Sam spots a note on the doormat.

"It's from the post person," Jo says. "They tried to deliver a package."

"Pop your shoes on, Sam. We'll go and collect it now, because it's something for you!"

"What is it?" Sam asks.

"You'll have to wait and see! But here's an idea – as we walk, why don't you create an algorithm of how we get to the post office?"

"Forward one, two, three," Sam counts the steps to the front gate and writes them down.

They turn right, and Sam starts counting again. "One, two, three …"

"Wait," says Jo. "We have to note down the right turn too. If you were explaining to someone how to get to the post office, you'd have to tell them when to turn. Computers are just the same – instructions have to be completely clear for them to be followed correctly."

They go another ten steps, then turn left,

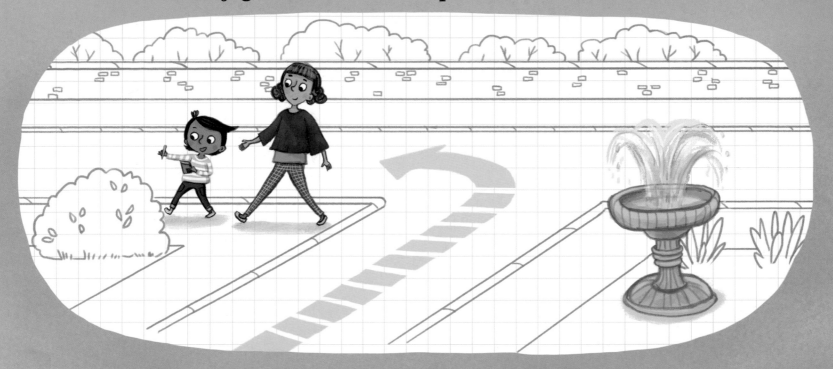

then walk forward four steps. They turn right,

but after five steps, there's a problem ...

There are builders digging up the road!

"We'll have to go back," says Jo.

"What about the post office?"

Jo smiles. "Bugs like this happen all the time in coding. But they always teach coders something useful. This road is shut, but we can get over this bug by working out a different way to the post office."

They go back five steps, then turn left instead of right at the junction.

They walk six steps, turn right,

go five steps forward and turn right again.

In eight more steps they're at the post office!

They return home with the package.

"Can I write out the code before I open it?" Sam asks.

"Of course!" Jo says.

"We could even send a robot to follow your algorithm to get to the post office," Jo tells Sam. "As long as it knew the meaning of the code."

"Could the robot go on its own?" Sam asks.

Jo nods. "We wouldn't need to be anywhere near it. Although it might give the post people a surprise!"

"People work with computers far away from them all the time — even as far as the moon and Mars!"

Margaret Heafield Hamilton led the team that wrote the code for the Apollo moon landings.

Without her software systems, Neil Armstrong and Buzz Aldrin might never have landed on the moon in 1969.

She also developed the software for America's first space station, Skylab.

Mars Rover

In more recent years, several robots have been sent to Mars, controlled by people back on Earth.

The robots have gathered information about rocks and soils on the planet to see whether its environment could support life.

"Wow!" Sam says. "Robots can do that?"

Jo grins. "They can do almost anything! Computers are becoming extremely intelligent and allowing us to do more and more."

Jo taps a little grey machine on the table and starts speaking to it. "Can you tell us about artificial intelligence?"

"Sure!" the box says in a robotic voice.

Artificial intelligence is the ability of a computer program or a machine to think and learn.

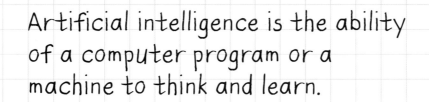

For example, self-driving cars learn how to drive so that a person doesn't have to.

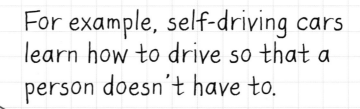

But it's vital they're safe and can cope with different weather and road conditions.

Some of the world's top coders are working on this, such as Tiancheng Lou, who co-founded China's most advanced self-driving company, Pony.ai.

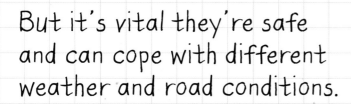

Sam opens the package. "A dog robot!"

"You can program it to do lots of things," Jo explains.

"So I'll need to learn its language!" Sam says, opening the box carefully and reading the instructions.

Soon Sam starts programming the robot dog
to bark something important to Auntie Jo ...

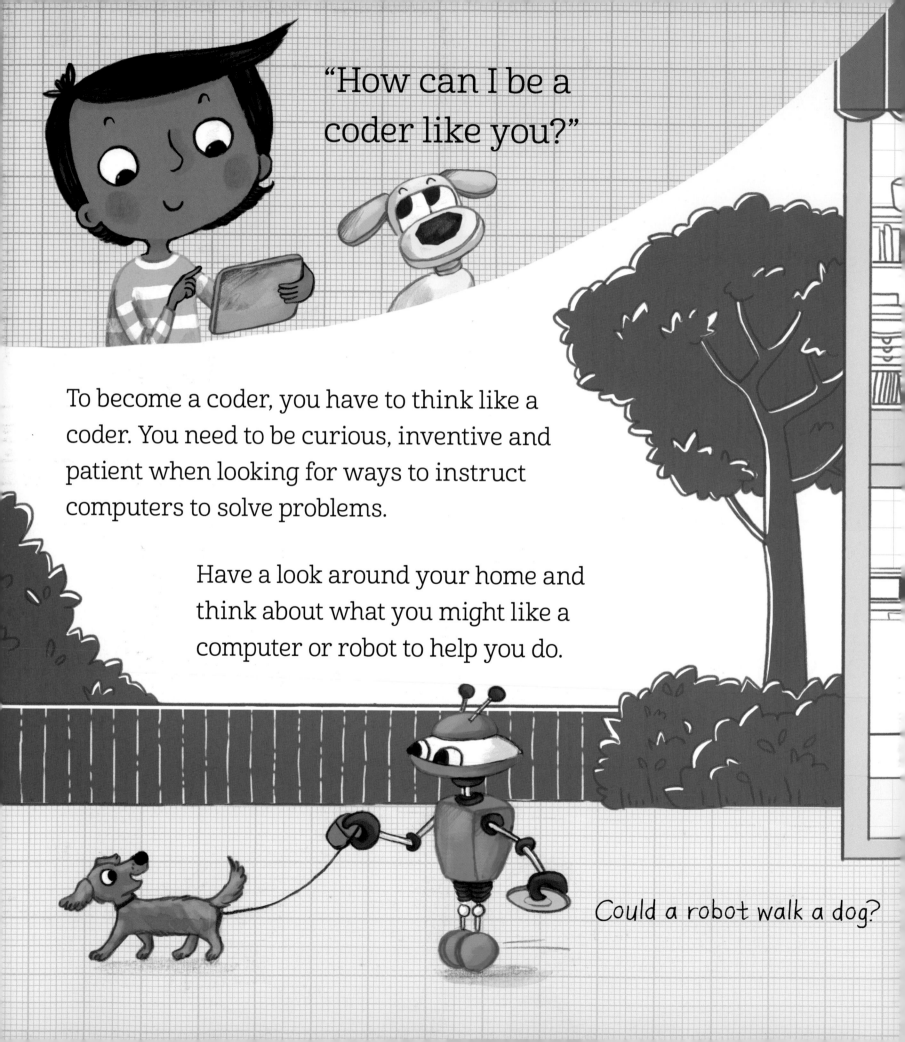

"How can I be a coder like you?"

To become a coder, you have to think like a coder. You need to be curious, inventive and patient when looking for ways to instruct computers to solve problems.

Have a look around your home and think about what you might like a computer or robot to help you do.

Could a robot walk a dog?

Could you design a new video game for your friends?

When it's time to sleep, could you program a lamp to switch off?

How could a robot help you pack your school bag?

How could a computer help you make art?

The best way to become a coder is to start learning the basics. The better you get at coding, the more creative ideas you can develop and see your code come to life!

How can you create code?

There are many ways you can learn how to code and one is through using ScratchJr. This is a free online programming language that can teach you coding skills.

Do you have a favourite story? Try using ScratchJr to create a short movie, animation or game based on your favourite story.

An important part of coding is to think about the steps your program must take. It's just like a story — a program goes from the beginning to the middle then to the end.

Putting coding steps in the right order is what coders call SEQUENCING. This series of steps makes up an ALGORITHM for the computer to use.

Remember, part of the fun of coding is finding and fixing mistakes, so don't worry if you mess up at first.

Ask a grown-up to sit with you when you visit www.scratchjr.org, then see what you can create together!

This book is dedicated to Mum, Dad, Sharlene
and especially Soraya, whose meticulous mind
was the inspiration for this book. Thanks to you all
for your support and love – S.S.

To my brother Ville, the best tech problem-solver and
computer builder a sister could ever have – N.S.

First published in Great Britain in 2021 by Wren & Rook

HB ISBN: 978 1 5263 6205 6
PB ISBN: 978 1 5263 6207 0
E-book ISBN: 978 1 5263 6206 3
10 9 8 7 6 5 4 3 2 1

MIX
Paper from
responsible sources
FSC® C104740

FSC
www.fsc.org

Wren & Rook
An imprint of
Hachette Children's Group
Part of Hodder & Stoughton
Carmelite House
50 Victoria Embankment
London EC4Y 0DZ

An Hachette UK Company
www.hachette.co.uk
www.hachettechildrens.co.uk

Publishing Director: Debbie Foy
Managing Editor: Liza Miller
Senior Editor: Sadie Smith
Art Director: Laura Hambleton
Designer: Barbara Ward

Printed in China